SnapShots

A Family Comedy in One Act

By Jean Klein

Published by Blue Moon Plays

For the Once-in-a-Lifetime Blue Moon Experience

Copyright © 2011, Jean Klein

All rights reserved.
Snapshots Copyright © Jean Klein 2011

CAUTION: Professionals and amateurs are hereby warned that performance of SNAPSHOTS, hereinafter known as Play, is subject to payment of a royalty unless written permission is given waiving such fee. The Play is fully protected under the copyright laws of the United States of America, and of all countries covered by the International Copyright Union (including the Dominion of Canada and the rest of the British Commonwealth), and of all countries covered by the Pan-American Copyright Convention, the Universal Copyright Convention, and the Berne Convention, and of all countries with which the United States has reciprocal copyright relations. All rights, including professional/amateur stage rights, motion picture, recitation, lecturing, public reading, radio broadcasting, television, video or sound recording, all other forms of mechanical or electronic reproduction, such as CD-ROM, CD-I, DVD, information storage and retrieval systems and photo-copying, and the rights of translation into foreign languages, are strictly reserved. Particular emphasis is placed upon the matter of readings, permission for which must be secured from the Author in writing.

Anyone receiving permission to produce the Play is required to give credit to the Author as sole and exclusive Author of the Play on the title page of all programs distributed in connection with performances of the Play and in all instances in which the title of the Play appears for purposes of advertising, publicizing or otherwise exploiting the Play and/or a production thereof. Author's name must be at least one-third the size of the title.

Publisher: Blue Moon Plays, LLC
1385 Fordham Road, Ste 105-279
Virginia Beach, VA 23464
Printed in the USA
ISBN: 978-1-943416-05-9

CHANGES TO SCRIPT

Copyright law prevents this script from being copied or altered in any way by any technical or digital means. There may be no changes made to the script including but not limited to casting or dialogue without permission of the publisher and/or playwright.

PERFORMANCE/READING OF SCRIPT

This script is licensed for production by blue moon plays. It may NOT be performed or read aloud in any way (with or without admission fees) in a classroom, around a table, in front of a non-paying audience without a performance fee, which varies.

For any performance, you must apply for and purchase performance rights: in class, in school, for educational purposes, for paying or nonpaying audiences of any size, as a concert reading or a staged reading.

Anyone receiving permission to produce the Play is required to give credit to the Author as sole and exclusive Author of the Play on the title page of all programs distributed in connection with performances of the Play and in all instances in which the title of the Play appears for purposes of advertising, publicizing or otherwise exploiting the Play and/or a production thereof. Author's name must be one-half the size of the title.

All performances and/or readings of this script, whether or not admission fees are required, must apply for and receive a Performance License. There is a flat 100 fee if you wish to live stream performance.

Special Considerations:
Small-group readings around a table or in the classroom:
- If you are planning to use this script FOR CLASSROOM USE, you must purchase scripts for the members of your class or group. These may be purchased as a downloadable PDF (class/group study pack) which may be printed for that class only.
- If you are a small group doing private play readings for YOUR OWN ENTERTAINMENT or for a SMALL SENIOR ACTIVITY GROUP, you must purchase the number or scripts required by the characters: these may be purchased as a multi-copy download which will give you a printable script that you may copy for that reading only.

Video Taping
One video tape may be made for archival purposes only.

Livestreaming
Livestreaming is permissible with an additional fee.

Digital versions cannot be added to a free or paid online library or website, in any format, with or without member access, without the publisher's permission.

<u>TO PERFORM THIS PLAY</u>

<u>You must buy sufficient scripts for the cast + 3, apply for performance rights, pay the performance fee, and receive a performance license.</u>

To purchase scripts:

- Purchase sufficient printed hard copies (one for each cast member, plus 3 for the crew) - an automatic 10 percent discount is applied to multiple printed hardcopies at the point of ordering.

  or

- Purchase a Multicopy PDF which allows you to print sufficient copies of this script (one for each cast member, plus 3 for the crew). Click Return to Merchant to download your printable PDF. A link to the download will also be emailed to you, along with a link to the application for performance license.

To apply for a Performance License, go to the Product Page of the play and fill out and submit the application form.

To pay the Performance Fee, simply pay the invoice you will be emailed when we receive your application for performance.

Your Performance License for your requested dates will be emailed to you.

All scripts and licenses shall be obtained at Blue Moon Plays at www.havescripts.com

If you wish to make changes in the script of any kind, you must receive permission from the publisher or the playwright. Permission is usually granted readily when schools or theaters face casting problems and the changes do not affect the quality or intent of the original.

**For information, visit www.havescripts.com;
email info@bluemoonplays.com
or call 757-816-1164**

For classroom use - select Class/Group Study
For performance - select MultiCopy PDF

Snapshots

The Cast:

Sy   a man (plays 30's to 60's)
Maggie   a woman (plays 20's to 50's)
A Man   any age

The Stage: There are three cubes which will represent a variety of things: a bench, a table, etc. One cube can serve as a prop table and hold a Yahrzeit candle, a phone, a picture album, etc. There is also a coat rack on which there are items of clothing which the characters will put on as they age. When the lights go up, MAGGIE is sitting on a bench. MAGGIE is young, in her mid-twenties, wearing a casual top and holding a rosary. Occasionally MAGGIE looks around as if expecting someone. Someone offstage coughs. MAGGIE looks around, expectantly and half-rises. SY enters, a little older than MAGGIE and dressed in a suit and tie;. MAGGIE sits and turns back, disappointed. They freeze for a moment as we hear the sound of a camera snap and possibly see a brief flash of light. SY drops a cigarette butt and puts it out with his foot before he continues walking. He has his head down and moves his lips as if rehearsing something. He trips over her feet.

SY: *Oy! Tsedreyt in kop [Se drayt in cop]*

MAGGIE: What did you call me?

SY: What? Oh, no, not you. I'm just, I don't know, I wasn't watching where I was going . . .

MAGGIE: Are you all right? You want to sit down? *(She moves over on the bench.)*

SY: I really don't have much time.

MAGGIE: I hope I don't, either.

(MAGGIE *continues with her rosary.*)

SY: Are you waiting for someone?

MAGGIE:
    (looking at a ring on her finger)
Yes. And no. If he comes, I'll have to answer a question.

SY: Do you have an answer?

MAGGIE: No. And it makes me nervous.

SY: Then the answer better be "no." Always say "no" when something gives you schpielkes [shpeelkiss]?

MAGGIE: Gives me what? I certainly don't have . . . What are speelkes?

SY: SCHPielkes. Jewish ants in the pants.

MAGGIE: Oh! (*pause*) What makes them Jewish?

SY: I don't know. Maybe they're circumcised. *(He looks at the rosary in her hands.)* You're not Jewish, are you?

MAGGIE: What gave you that clue?

SY: Things just come to me sometimes.

MAGGIE: Like what?

SY: I don't know. Like auras, or just a change in the way the light falls across someone's face. It's hard to explain.

MAGGIE: I understand. I was born with a caul [cowl] over my face. My grandmother said that meant I had second sight.

SY: And do you?

MAGGIE: *(looking at ring)* Never when I need it.

SY: We ought to get together sometime. I teach over at the University.

MAGGIE: Oh! Me, too! I just started

        (SY looks at his watch.)

MAGGIE: You have to go?

SY: You don't want me here for your big scene.

MAGGIE: It might not hurt.

SY: Sorry. I've got my own big scene.

        (They freeze as we hear/see the camera flash. SY turns and leaves her and goes to the prop cube where there is an unlit Yarzheit candle and the photo album. SY turns a page in the album, takes a cigarette from his pocket, pats himself for a match and finds none. He tosses the cigarette, looks off stage, and pulls a yarmulke from his other pocket and puts it on. A VOICE calls from off-stage.)

VOICE: Sy, is that you? We've been waiting.

SY: *(calling offstage)* I'm here.

VOICE: Pops knew you'd be late. He put it in the will to wait for you. We went ahead and covered the mirrors. Hurry up! We need ten men.

SY: Don't you have a minyan?

VOICE: We will when you get here.

> (SY exits, carrying the candle with him. Offstage we hear the sounds of the beginning of Kaddish. [A sample of two prayers is attached at the end; these should be intoned or chanted. Samples of cantors performing the Kaddish are available on the Internet, one of which can be found at http://www.jewfaq.org/prayer/kaddish.htm
>
> MAGGIE rises and paces, looks around, takes a ring off her finger and places it carefully on the cube. MAGGIE exits. The MAN as a park attendant enters, carrying a leaf bag over his shoulder. He finds the ring on the bench and holds it up to the light. SY enters, taking off his yarmulke and putting it in his pocket. SY stares at the MAN and the ring.)

MAN: *(about to put ring in his pocket)* You know who this belongs to?

SY: Yeah. She must've left it. How about that?

MAN: I'll put it in the lost and found.

SY: But I'll probably see her . . .

MAN: Everything I find goes in the lost and found.

SY: What if it's neither lost nor found?

MAN: In my job, there's no either/or. Everything's lost or found.

SY: Okay, then, that ring's *both* lost and found. She lost it and you found it.

MAN: Are you trying to drive me nuts?

SY: No, it's just that I like words to be used precisely—

MAN: Hoo-boy. A thing is lost or it is found. No middle ground. That's the way I like things.

SY: That's a very simplistic view of the world.

MAN: Thank you.

SY: That wasn't how I meant it.

MAN: What you meant is irrelevant. It's all in how I take it.

SY: *(pause)* Now, you're driving me nuts. You ever been a rabbi?

MAN: Nope. Jesuit.

(The MAN puts the ring in his pocket.)

SY: Same thing. I'll tell her you found the ring.

MAN: If she ever needs it, I'll make sure she gets it.

(SY exits. The MAN takes a lamp and a phone out of the bag and places them on the appropriate cube, moves the bench back, mimes picking up some trash, looks around and exits. The lights dim to suggest night.

(SY enters, wearing a different jacket and carrying a briefcase. He turns on the lamp; lights rise. The implication is that he is returning home for the day. He removes his jacket and hangs it on the clothes tree. He keeps picking up his watch and glancing at the phone. He places a cigarette in his mouth, but before he can light it, the phone rings. SY puts the cigarette in his pocket and picks the phone up quickly, facing stage right.)

SY: Yeah? What? Where are you? You were supposed to call at three.

(MAGGIE enters, stage left, holding a phone with the receiver to her ear.. MAGGIE is now wearing a lightweight suit jacket and perhaps has her hair pulled back.)

MAGGIE: I went to visit my mother.

SY: I knew it. I had a feeling . . .

MAGGIE: Would you stop it with the feelings? You think I'm going to consult you before I go somewhere to see if it's safe?

SY: So, you're okay?

MAGGIE: Of course, I'm okay

SY: And nothing happened.

MAGGIE: Not really, *(pause)* well . . . I had an accident . . .

SY: I told you I was nervous about that trip . . .

MAGGIE: I know. I know. But you're always nervous about something.

SY: Well, I was right, wasn't I?

MAGGIE: It was a fender bender!

SY: So, I didn't say you'd be mangled. You shouldn't have gone up there today. There was too much ice on the road.

MAGGIE: It was even icier in my mom's house. I finally told her I wasn't engaged any longer.

SY: It took you three months to tell her that?

MAGGIE: She liked Bruce.

SY: That was his name?

MAGGIE: Bruce McIntyre.

SY: I can guess that he wasn't Jewish either.

MAGGIE: I wish I'd waited another three months. You should have heard her. "You're just too picky. You'll never find anyone at your age. What am I going to tell your Aunt Mary?"

SY: You want to get married?

MAGGIE: Are you asking?

SY: I don't know. Are you answering?

MAGGIE: That depends.

SY: On what?

MAGGIE: On what you're asking.

SY: That depends.

MAGGIE: On what?

SY: On what you're answering.

MAGGIE: Are we going to keep going round and round like this?

SY: It depends.

MAGGIE: Oh, no. Not again!

SY: Why not? (pause) You and me. That would really drive your mother meshugeh [*ma-shoog-uh*].

MAGGIE: Well, it depends.

SY: Now, you're starting?

MAGGIE: Only if you stop smoking. I'd never marry anyone who smokes

SY: Then I guess the wedding's off. (pause) Are you sure you're all right?

MAGGIE: Sure. (*pause*) Were you worried about me?

SY: I worry about everything, remember?

MAGGIE: So, I guess it's no trouble to add me to the list.

SY: Look, I'm sorry. I didn't want to be right.

MAGGIE: (*jokingly*) Uh-huh

SY: Really. Look. You want me to come over? I could bring you some soup or something. Make you a Reuben? Sure you don't need me?

MAGGIE: Not tonight. I've got all those freshmen scheduled for conferences tomorrow . . .

SY: Okay. Uh . . . I've got tickets for *The Turn of the Screw* for Sunday matinee.

MAGGIE: The opera?

SY: You want to go? We both have to teach it this semester.

MAGGIE: Sunday? Sure, why not?

(*SY holds the receiver up triumphantly.*)

SY: Yes!

(*MAGGIE hangs up her phone.*)

MAGGIE: When am going to get the guts to tell him I hate opera?

(*MAGGIE shakes her head at the phone. SY picks up his briefcase, a stack of papers and a cigarette which he dangles from his lips. They freeze for a moment and there is the sound and light of the camera flash. They exit, taking the phone, briefcase, etc., with them as they go, SY turning a page in the photo album as he crosses.*

The scene changes to the park. There is the faint sound of Muzetta's Waltz in background. The MAN enters carrying a broom and radio which is playing Muzetta's Waltz. Music up. He places the radio on a cube and moves the bench back to its original position. MAGGIE enters and sits on the bench and opens a book which she continues to read.

SY enters and stands for a moment in the background. The MAN crosses to him and hands him a box of Crackerjack.

SY: Thanks. What's this for?

MAN: Nothing. It's from me to you.

SY: These were my favorite as a kid.

MAN: Mine, too. You never know what the surprise was going to be.

(The MAN exits, taking his radio and the lamp. Music fades SY enters, eating crackerjack. He takes a bite or two throughout the scene.)

SY: I thought I'd find you here. Crackerjack. Want some?

MAGGIE: I thought you had class, now.

SY: I do. I'm making them listen to *The Turn of the Screw*. I told you that could do double duty. You want it next week?

MAGGIE: Oh, sure. This is your third year, right?

SY: And my last, apparently.

MAGGIE: You didn't get tenure track? Why? *(He shrugs.)* What're you going to do?

SY: Go back east, I guess. Finish my dissertation. Something like that.

MAGGIE: What are you going to tell all those women?

SY: What women?

MAGGIE: The one who cleans for you on Monday. The one who cooks on Tuesday. Etc.

SY: I didn't think you knew about them.

MAGGIE: You'd be surprised what I know.

SY: Do you mind about them?

MAGGIE: Not really.

SY: (*disappointed*) Oh. That's very flattering.

MAGGIE: They always seemed kind of interchangeable to me. Defined by the tasks they did.

SY: Yeah. I never quite knew what to do with you.

MAGGIE: So I ended up on Sunday

SY: It's only Sundays that give me a problem.

MAGGIE: Yeah, it looks like I might have to start worrying about my Sundays, too. (*Pause*) Why was I always on Sundays?

SY: Don't know. You were different I guess. I kind of felt sorry for you.

MAGGIE: Sorry for me!

SY: In a good way.

MAGGIE: There's a *good* way?

SY: I think so. Like I feel sorry for myself sometimes. Especially on Sundays. That's a hard day to be single. You just want somebody at home. Maybe that's why you never did anything for me. Like the cooking. Or the laundry.

MAGGIE: Damned right I didn't.

SY: You mean if we were married, you wouldn't get up in the morning and make me breakfast?

MAGGIE: I can't even make myself breakfast.

SY: My mother went to the deli every morning and got Pops fresh bagels. That's what he missed the most when she died.

MAGGIE: Why didn't he get them himself?

SY: He didn't know where the store was.

MAGGIE: Oy, veh! *(She obviously practicing her Yiddish and doesn't get it quite right.)* A Farbissoner (far-*biss*-on-er)

SY: .Now you're talking like an educated person. (*pause*) Almost. *(He takes something out of the box.)* Look what I found!

(SY holds up the ring and looks at it.)

MAGGIE: Wow, pretty nice for a box of crackerjack. I had a ring almost like this, once. What's that doing in a crackerjack box?

SY: I don't know. Maybe someone put it there on purpose? He meant to propose and lost his nerve. Or maybe someone didn't show up?

MAGGIE: I've known that to happen.

SY: Showing up is important.

MAGGIE: Yeah, it is. You always do that, show up when you say you will.

SY: *(looking at ring)* I try. I wonder what kind of wedding they would have had.

MAGGIE: I don't know. (pause) I don't like big weddings.

SY: Nah. They make me nervous. God. Like big Jewish weddings. And big Jewish bar mitzvah's. Small would be best, don't you think? In December?

MAGGIE: Yeah. December's a good month for weddings.

(The MAN calls from backstage.)

MAN: Park's closing in a few.

(SY stands and hesitates, looking back and forth between the ring and MAGGIE. Finally he places the ring on the bench.)

SY: I guess we should leave this for whoever it belongs to? Okay. You want to go over to Gazebo? They've got great pastrami. I think they're still serving lunch.

MAGGIE: *(glancing at the ring)* You mean it?

SY: Yeah, why?

MAGGIE: Uh . . . It's not Sunday.

SY: Somewhere in the world it's Sunday.

MAGGIE: No, it isn't. That's only for the time. Like, somewhere in the world it's 5 o'clock—

SY: It could be true for Sunday, too? Who knows? There's an exception for everything.

MAGGIE: I guess there is. I'll meet you there. I've got my car parked on the campus.

SY: Okay.

> *(SY exits. MAGGIE looks at the ring, picks it up, studies it, and puts it in her pocket. SY enters again.)*

SY: I forgot. I don't have a car. Can you give me a ride?

MAGGIE: Don't I always?

> *(They exit together. The MAN enters with champagne glass, sees that the ring is gone, raises his glass, and freezes to the click/sound of the camera. From offstage there is the sound of the Wedding March which quickly turns into Have Negillah to which the MAN does the hora and dances off-stage. Music off.*
>
> *MAGGIE enters wearing a sweatshirt with a laptop which she places on the cube beside the papers. She types. SY enters, turns a page in the photo album, and looks around.)*

SY: Just look at this place.

MAGGIE: What's wrong with it?

SY: Look at all that bubbeleh [*boob*-uh-luh) on the floor? *(He stoops and picks up something small from the floor and inspects it microscopically.)* And the dust?

MAGGIE: I don't see dust.

SY: How can you not see dust? Look! It's right there.

MAGGIE: It must be congenital. Anyway, It makes life easier. Besides, I thought you dusted.

SY: I do. Because you don't! According to you, you have a rare form of astigmatism which blocks out dust and spilled coffee and . . .

MAGGIE: Exactly. So. why should I clean what I can't see? You don't like the way I do anything. I vacuumed once—

SY: And you didn't get the lines in the rug straight. If they're crooked, what's the point of vacuuming? And besides, it's a carpet, not a rug.

MAGGIE: For God's sake, what's the difference?

SY: Rugs are smaller than carpets. Rugs do not usually exceed the length of 2m (6.5ft). They usually have multiple uses. They may be used as centerpiece flooring, or hung on wall. They may be used as foot rugs sofa or bed throws or as table decor. They usually have an artistic or stylish touch in terms of patterns, shape—

MAGGIE: You have more useless information in your head than ten Encyclopedias—and please don't start to tell me how that's different from an Atlas, or a compendium, or—

SY: Can I help it my mother always made me read?

MAGGIE: Your mother! Thank God she didn't live to see you marry a shiksa.

> (SY mimes throwing out the speck he's been holding in the garbage. He peers down as if into the garbage can. They become increasingly irritated with one another.)

SY: There's garbage in here.

MAGGIE: It's a garbage can.

SY: But it's coffee grounds. Wet garbage goes in the empty milk container.

MAGGIE: I couldn't find an empty one!

SY: Then use a baggie!

MAGGIE:
I can't remember all your rules for how to throw out the garbage. Are they somewhere in the Talmud?

SY: Those have nothing to do with my religion. Which, as you may have noticed, I've stopped practicing. (pause) Thanks to you.

MAGGIE: You stopped going to schul two years before I met you! And how long has it been since I've been to Mass?

SY: Did I stop you?

MAGGIE: No! But I have to spend so much time figuring out your garbage rules—

SY: Well, you don't go to Mass, you go to Hell. I don't go to schul, well, I probably get a pass. Some rules just make sense.

MAGGIE: Sense!   One kind of bag for coffee grounds. Another for potato peels. And a jar for chicken fat. And God forbid if I should put either of those actually in the garbage can itself! Sometimes I think you married me just so you could boss me around.

SY: Hah! Well, if I'm so bossy, why'd you marry me?

MAGGIE: Because you told me to!

SY: You don't have to listen to everything I say!

MAGGIE: Says you! I don't think you listen to *anything* I say!

SY: Just look around this place! I don't even have a Kosher kitchen.

MAGGIE: I got news for you, buddy. You don't even have a Kosher wife.

> *(They stop and stare at one another then burst out laughing. There is the sound of a baby crying from next door. They listen.)*

SY: Sounds like the Rosens next door got home from the hospital.

MAGGIE: Sounds like it.

SY: Oy, another bar mitzvah in thirteen years.

MAGGIE: That's a long time.

SY: You'll be surprised how fast it gets here.

MAGGIE: Why did you marry me, Sy?

SY: Let's say I just had a slight lapse of judgement.

MAGGIE: Really, Sy. Why?

SY: (pause) You were the only one who never took care of me. You wanted me to do things for you.

MAGGIE: Come on. Really.

SY: Sometimes things that scared the hell out of me—

MAGGIE: Like getting married.

SY: Yeah, kind of like that. (pause) And you made Sundays bearable.

MAGGIE: What about the rest of the week?

SY: Don't push it. By me, one out of seven's pretty good. (*covering his ears*) *How* long do they cry like that?

MAGGIE: Got me. I was an only child. Maybe one day, we'll find out.

> (*MAGGIE exits. The baby cries again. SY sits on a cube with his ears covered. Gradually the cries cease and he uncovers his ears, pushes the buttons of an imaginary stereo, listening to the male duet from The Pearl Fishers. Lights dim as if time passes.*
>
> *MAGGIE enters, wearing a maternity smock. She is close to due. She freezes and the camera clicks. She turns a page in the photo album.*}

MAGGIE
You haven't played that in a long time.

(SY listens for a moment, then turns it off.)

MAGGIE: Why did you do that?

SY: You missed the beginning. If you care about music, you're careful with how you listen to it. You have to hear all the notes.

MAGGIE: That doesn't make sense.

SY: Nu? It has to make sense? I don't like it when you pop in and out like you only want to hear the parts you like, as if the rest of the music didn't matter. You can't be careless with things that matter. Like a baby?

(MAGGIE storms off. The MAN appears in a spot on the edge of the stage, wearing a stethoscope and a scrub cap.)

SY: *(crossing to the MAN)* Oh, God, what am I going to do with a baby. I hope it's a girl. Girls always love their daddies. I won't be as afraid of a girl.

MAN: It's a boy, Sy. Look. A big boy. You'll be proud of him, but you'll never understand him. That's just the way it goes.

(They freeze to the sound of a camera. They exit. MAGGIE enters, turning a page in the photo album. She looks around.)

MAGGIE: Sy? Sy! It's time for Manny's game! *(There is a blast of music from off-stage.)* Oh, God, he's taping again.

(The MAN enters, wearing a baseball cap and carrying a bat. He is now playing the son, Manny, a young teenager.)

MAN: Thanks for pitching to me yesterday, Mom. I think my swing's slot better.

MAGGIE: Well, my mom was on one of the first women's leagues. I guess she taught me something. (pause) I never did tell her that.

MAN: Is Dad going today? He said he might.

MAGGIE: (*looking upward at the music*) He said he'd be along later.

MAN: I know. That's what he always says.

MAGGIE: Hurry up, now!

MAN: Be right there.

> (*MAGGIE exits. MAN stops for a moment.*

MAN: Dad? (pause) Dad?

> (*The music rises: The Pearl Fisher duet. The MAN mimes a swing and a hit, watching the ball go out of the park. The music rises as the MAN looks up.*)

MAGGIE (OS): Manny? Hurry up!

MAN: I'm coming.

> (*He exits. The music abruptly stops as the sounds of Take Me Out to the Ball Game rise and fade.*)
>
> *In a moment, SY enters with a cane, wearing glasses. MAGGIE enters behind him, carrying a suitcase.*)

MAGGIE: I guess he's about ready to go.

SY: You sure he's got his plane ticket?

MAGGIE: Yeah. I'll just take this suitcase out.

SY: And clean underwear? You can never have enough –

MAGGIE: He knows how to use the washer and dryer—

SY: And clean shirts?

MAGGIE: He can iron, too—God knows, how. I don't touch anything but wash and wear—

SY: I've noticed.

> *(MAGGIE exits. MAN enters, wearing different cap and carrying a suitcase.)*

MAN: It's time for me to go, Dad.

SY: Whatever. You don't come back with less than a B

MAN: I wouldn't dare.

SY: That's what you told me in high school. It didn't help. You always came back.

MAN: *(teasing)* I just couldn't stay away from you.

SY: That's what they say about fathers and sons. *(pause)* I wish I'd been more. . . . You know . . .

MAN: Yeah. Me, too. *(SY reaches in his pocket.)* Here. Take this with you.

> (*He puts something in his hand. The MAN inspects it.*)

MAN
A quarter?

SY
It's a lucky one. I found it on the street yesterday. Luck you'll need more than money.

> (*MAGGIE enters.*)

MAGGIE: You about ready? (*MAN nods.*) Sy, you coming to the airport?

> (*SY looks back and forth between them.*)

MAN: He doesn't have to, Mom. The opera's about to come on. You know he needs to tape it.

MAGGIE: The opera. Always the opera.

SY: I married you because you loved the opera.

MAGGIE: I guess you don't always get what you pay for.

SY: Did you?

MAGGIE: It's too soon to tell.

> (*They freeze—sound and light of camera. MAGGIE and MAN exit, MAGGIE turning a page in the album as they go. SY turns on the opera—Muzetta's Waltz is playing.*)

MAGGIE: Hell, Sy, don't you care about anything but the opera?

SY: Now, what? *(SY quickly turns it off.)*

MAGGIE: I know. I know. I missed some notes. You've missed more than that,

SY: You're telling me?!

MAGGIE: What's that supposed to mean?

SY: Nothing, Maggie. With you, nothing can ever be simple.

MAGGIE: And you're the epitome of simplicity? How long have we been married?

SY: Don't ask.

MAGGIE: You don't remember!

SY: Do you?

MAGGIE: I remember that you never said you loved me.

SY: Sure, I did.

MAGGIE: When?

SY
Whenever I turned the music on.

MAGGIE
Oh! But what about when you turn it off?

SY: You complained about my taping so much, I thought it bothered you.

MAGGIE: Oh. It never did.

(She crosses and turns the music back on very low.)

MAGGIE: This house is going to feel very empty.

SY: It's been empty for a long time.

MAGGIE: I wish you hadn't said that.

SY: You see? You always want to talk and then you don't like what you hear.

MAGGIE: Did you mean that, Sy? Did you really mean it?

SY: Oh, Maggie. Have you looked at my driver's license?

MAGGIE: What?

SY: They took my picture this time. I look old. Like an old man. I don't know what I mean by anything. Sometimes I think we don't match.

MAGGIE: Are you just coming to that conclusion?

SY: No. (*pause*) Manny's not Jewish, you know.

MAGGIE: Mama's baby, Papa's maybe? I offered to convert. Before he was born.

SY: You wouldn't have liked it. The mikvah.

MAGGIE: The idea of a communal bath never appealed to me. But . . .It's not too late.

SY: I guess it's not too necessary either.

MAGGIE: But it's something to think about.

SY: Yeah. One of these days. (pause) Maybe I'll go out to the garden. I want to do some weeding.

MAGGIE: You want to have a cigarette.

SY: Well, you won't let me smoke in here.

MAGGIE: Well, now that Manny's gone . . .I guess you can.

 (She takes an ashtray from a cube.)

SY: You still have this?

MAGGIE: I didn't have the heart to throw every ashtray away . . . Or ban them from the house.

SY: One of my few pleasures over the years. I bought this in Mexico—so many years ago. My one sabbatical.

MAGGIE: Did you go alone?

SY: No.

MAGGIE: I see. (She stoops to pick something off the rug.) Maybe we could go there. Now that we have more time . . .

SY: It's too late for that. I've grown used to being who I am

 (SY picks up a Yarzheit candle from a cube.)

MAGGIE: What are you doing with that?

SY: I don't know. I bought it the other day. I thought it would be a good idea to have one. Just in case.

MAGGIE: You expecting someone to die?

SY: Well, you never know. When we were at the store the other day, it just came to me that it would be a good thing to have. (pause) You remember where that CD is? Vivaldi's Gloria?

MAGGIE: It's on the bookcase.

SY: You remember, that's what I want to have played. Not the Mozart. The Vivaldi.

MAGGIE: Do you know something I don't?

SY: If I did, would I be able to tell you?

MAGGIE: Damn it, Sy. You and your "feelings." Every time you look at me, I'm afraid you're going to see aura around my head or something.

SY: Oh, Maggie, they were guesses. You were in an accident. Your mother died after I complained it was cold in the house—

MAGGIE: After you told me to see her one last time—

SY: I didn't put it that way—

MAGGIE: Yes, you did. And when I lost the baby—

SY: It's better not to talk about that. It was what I felt, not what I wanted. (pause) Manny will be fine, if that's what's worrying you.

MAGGIE: It wasn't.

SY: I'm not sorry about any of it.

MAGGIE: Would you do it again?

SY: (pause and smiles) Don't push your luck. I was wrong, sometimes, too.

> *SY crosses to the other cube, puts the Yarzheit candle on it and exits.)*

MAGGIE: No, you weren't, Sy. You were never wrong. Not about anything that counted.

> *MAGGIE crosses to the Yarzheit candle. She has her rosary. The MAN as the son joins her.)*

MAGGIE: They haven't started yet.

MAN: Maybe they need a minyan.

MAGGIE: But you can't—You never learned—

> *(MAN crosses and takes a yarmulke from the stand and puts it on his head.*

MAN
Maybe I can. Some things are just in the blood.

> *(He lights the Yahrzeit candle.)*

MAGGIE: You know what to do?

MAN: Pop had his stereo. I have the Internet.

MAGGIE: Thank God he never learned to use the Internet. He would have bought out EBay. Oh, Manny, who's gonna tell me what to do now?

VOICE: We're waiting.

MAN: Do you have a minyan?

VOICE: We will when you get here.

(The sound and light of the final snapshot. The MAN turns the final page in the photo album as he exits.)

CURTAIN

PRAYERS FOR FIRST SCENE

EL MOLE RACHAMIM

Exalted, compassionate God, grant perfect peace in Your sheltering Presence, among the holy and the pure, to the souls of all our beloved who have gone to their eternal home. May their memory endure as inspiration for deeds of charity and goodness in our lives. May their souls thus be bound up in the bond of life. May they rest in peace. And let us say: Amen.

KADDISH

Yit'gadal v'yit'kadash sh'mei raba (Cong: Amein).
May His great Name grow exalted and sanctified (`Cong: Amen.)

b'al'ma di v'ra khir'utei
in the world that He created as He willed.

v'yam'likh mal'khutei b'chayeikhon uv'yomeikhon
May He give reign to His kingship in your lifetimes and in your days,

uv'chayei d'khol beit yis'ra'eil
and in the lifetimes of the entire Family of Israel,

ba'agala uviz'man kariv v'im'ru:
swiftly and soon. Now say:
(Mourners and Congregation:)

Amein. Y'hei sh'mei raba m'varakh l'alam ul'al'mei al'maya
(Amen. May His great Name be blessed forever and ever.)

Yit'barakh v'yish'tabach v'yit'pa'ar v'yit'romam v'yit'nasei
Blessed, praised, glorified, exalted, extolled,

v'yit'hadar v'yit'aleh v'yit'halal sh'mei d'kud'sha
mighty, upraised, and lauded be the Name of the Holy One

(Mourners and Congregation:)

B'rikh hu.
Blessed is He.

l'eila min kol bir'khata v'shirara
beyond any blessing and song,

toosh'b'chatah v'nechematah, da'ameeran b'al'mah, v'eemru:
praise and consolation that are uttered in the world. Now say:
(Mourners and Congregation:)

Amein
Amen

Y'hei sh'lama raba min sh'maya
May there be abundant peace from Heaven

v'chayim aleinu v'al kol yis'ra'eil v'im'ru
and life upon us and upon all Israel. Now say:
(Mourners and Congregation:)

Amein
Amen

Oseh shalom bim'romav hu ya'aseh shalom
He Who makes peace in His heights, may He make peace,

aleinu v'al kol Yis'ra'eil v'im'ru
upon us and upon all Israel. Now say:
(Mourners and Congregation:)

Amein
Amen

www.ingramcontent.com/pod-product-compliance
Lightning Source LLC
Chambersburg PA
CBHW071803040426
42446CB00012B/2695